THE
RULE OF
ST BENEDICT

THE RULE OF ST BENEDICT

SIRIUS

Disclaimer

Throughout the text readers may find that some of the language used and sentiments expressed are unacceptable by today's standards. These reflect the attitudes and usage common at the time the book was written. In no way do they reflect the attitude of the publishers.

Based on the standard translation by Leonard J. Doyle.

This edition published in 2024 by Sirius Publishing, a division of Arcturus Publishing Limited,
26/27 Bickels Yard, 151–153 Bermondsey Street,
London SE1 3HA

ISBN: 978-1-3988-4337-0
AD011473UK

Printed in China

CONTENTS

Introduction 11

Prologue 13

1. On the Kinds of Monks 19
2. What Kind of Man the Abbot Ought
   to Be 21
3. On Calling the Brethren for Counsel 27
4. What Are the Instruments of
   Good Works 29
5. On Obedience 35
6. On the Spirit of Silence 39
7. On Humility 41
8. On the Divine Office During the Night 51
9. How Many Psalms Are to Be Said
   at the Night Office 53
10. How the Night Office Is to Be Said
    in Summer Time 55
11. How the Night Office Is to Be Said
    on Sundays 57
12. How the Morning Office Is to Be Said 59
13. How the Morning Office Is to Be Said
    on Weekdays 61
14. How the Night Office Is to Be Said
    on the Feasts of the Saints 63
15. At What Times "Alleluia" Is to Be Said 65
16. How the Work of God Is to Be
    Performed During the Day 67
17. How Many Psalms Are to Be Said
    at These Hours 69
18. In What Order the Psalms Are to
    Be Said 71

19. On the Manner of Saying the Divine Office 75
20. On Reverence in Prayer 77
21. On the Deans of the Monastery 79
22. How the Monks Are to Sleep 81
23. On Excommunication for Faults 83
24. What the Measure of Excommunication Should Be 85
25. On Weightier Faults 87
26. On Those Who Without an Order Associate With the Excommunicated 89
27. How Solicitous the Abbot Should Be for the Excommunicated 91
28. On Those Who Will Not Amend After Repeated Corrections 93
29. Whether Brethren Who Leave the Monastery Should Be Received Again 95
30. How Boys Are to Be Corrected 97
31. What Kind of Man the Cellarer of the Monastery Should Be 99
32. On the Tools and Property of the Monastery 103
33. Whether Monks Ought to Have Anything of Their Own 105
34. Whether All Should Receive in Equal Measure What Is Necessary 107
35. On the Weekly Servers in the Kitchen 109
36. On the Sick Brethren 113
37. On Old Men and Children 115
38. On the Weekly Reader 117
39. On the Measure of Food 119
40. On the Measure of Drink 121
41. At What Hours the Meals Should Be Taken 123

42. That No One Speak After Compline........125

43. On Those Who Come Late to the
    Work of God or to Table............................127

44. How the Excommunicated Are to
    Make Satisfaction 131

45. On Those Who Make Mistakes in the
    Oratory...133

46. On Those Who Fail in Any Other
    Matters 135

47. On Giving the Signal for the Time
    of the Work of God 137

48. On the Daily Manual Labor........................139

49. On the Observance of Lent 143

50. On Brethren Who Are Working Far
    From the Oratory or Are on a Journey...145

51. On Brethren Who Go Not Very
    Far Away 147

52. On the Oratory of the Monastery...........149

53. On the Reception of Guests 151

54. Whether a Monk Should Receive
    Letters or Anything Else............................155

55. On the Clothes and Shoes of
    the Brethren.. 157

56. On the Abbot's Table 161

57. On the Craftsmen of the Monastery.......163

58. On the Manner of Receiving Brethren ...165

59. On the Sons of Nobles and of the Poor
    Who Are Offered 169

60. On Priests Who May Wish to Live in
    the Monastery 171

61. How Pilgrim Monks Are To Be
    Received 173

62. On the Priests of the Monastery.............177

63. On the Order of the Community............179

64. On Constituting an Abbot.....................183

65. On the Prior of the Monastery............187

66. On the Porters of the Monastery.........191

67. On Brethren Who Are Sent on
    a Journey...193

68. If a Brother Is Commanded to Do
    Impossible Things 195

69. That the Monks Presume Not to
    Defend One Another 197

70. That No One Venture to Punish at
    Random 199

71. That the Brethren Be Obedient to
    One Another 201

72. On the Good Zeal Which Monks
    Ought to Have 203

73. On the Fact That the Full Observance
    of Justice Is Not Established in
    This Rule...205

The dates inserted in the text are to point that portion of the Rule which is read in monasteries every day, either at Prime, or if it be a fast day, before the evening collation. The entire Rule is thus read through three times each year.

INTRODUCTION

St. Benedict, the patron saint of Europe, was born in 480 CE in Nursia, Italy. He is renowned as the pioneer of Western monasticism. No records remain of his early life, but his devotion to prayer and reflection as a young man led him to a hermitage in Subiaco, where he attracted many followers due to his legendary piety.

As he neared middle age, Benedict established the Monte Cassino monastery, where he authored *The Rule of Saint Benedict*, a guidebook to life advocating for moderation, prayer, work, and community living. Due to a papal endorsement, this Rule became the cornerstone of the Benedictine Order, influencing monastic life across Europe.

Benedict's teachings centered on "ora et labora"—balancing prayer and work—and emphasized humility, obedience, and structured living within monasteries. Monte Cassino became a hub for learning, spirituality, and hospitality under his guidance.

St. Benedict died around 547 CE, leaving a lasting legacy. Canonized by the Catholic Church, he is still revered for his wisdom, spiritual teachings, and contribution to structured communal living. His Rule remains a timeless guide for those wishing to lead a purposeful and balanced life. Today his Rule is read in monasteries daily—with dates given for when to read which passage—meaning that the entire book is read three times a year.

PROLOGUE

Jan. 1—May 2—Sept. 1

Listen, my son, to your master's precepts, and incline the ear of your heart. Receive willingly and carry out effectively your loving father's advice, that by the labor of obedience you may return to Him from whom you had departed by the sloth of disobedience.

To you, therefore, my words are now addressed, whoever you may be, who are renouncing your own will to do battle under the Lord Christ, the true King, and are taking up the strong, bright weapons of obedience.

And first of all, whatever good work you begin to do, beg of Him with most earnest prayer to perfect it, that He who has now deigned to count us among His sons may not at any time be grieved by our evil deeds. For we must always so serve Him with the good things He has given us, that He will never as an angry Father disinherit His children, nor ever as a dread Lord, provoked by our evil actions, deliver us to everlasting punishment as wicked servants who would not follow Him to glory.

Jan. 2—May 3—Sept. 2

Let us arise, then, at last, for the Scripture stirs us up, saying, "Now is the hour for us to rise from sleep." Let us open our eyes to the deifying light, let us hear with attentive ears the warning which the divine voice cries daily to us, "Today if you hear His voice, harden not your hearts." And again, "He who has ears to hear, let him hear what the Spirit says to the churches." And what does He say? "Come, My children, listen to Me; I will teach you the fear of the Lord. Run while you have the light of life, lest the darkness of death overtake you."

Jan. 3—May 4—Sept. 3

And the Lord, seeking His laborer in the multitude to whom He thus cries out, says again, "Who is the man who will have life, and desires to see good days?" And if, hearing Him, you answer, "I am he," God says to you, "If you will have true and everlasting life, keep your tongue from evil and your lips that they speak no guile. Turn away from evil and do good; seek after peace and pursue it. And when you have done these things, My eyes shall be upon you and My ears open to your prayers; and before you call upon Me, I will say to you, 'Behold, here I am.'"

What can be sweeter to us, dear brethren, than this voice of the Lord inviting us? Behold, in His loving kindness the Lord shows us the way of life.

Jan. 4—May 5—Sept. 4

Having our loins girded, therefore, with faith and the performance of good works, let us walk in His paths by the guidance of the Gospel, that we may deserve to see Him who has called us to His kingdom.

For if we wish to dwell in the tent of that kingdom, we must run to it by good deeds or we shall never reach it.

But let us ask the Lord, with the Prophet, "Lord, who shall dwell in Your tent, or who shall rest upon Your holy mountain?"

After this question, brethren, let us listen to the Lord as He answers and shows us the way to that tent, saying, "He who walks without stain and practices justice; he who speaks truth from his heart; he who has not used his tongue for deceit; he who has done no evil to his neighbor; he who has given no place to slander against his neighbor."

It is he who, under any temptation from the malicious devil, has brought him to naught by casting him and his temptation from the sight of his heart; and who has laid hold of his thoughts while they were still young and dashed them against Christ.

It is they who, fearing the Lord, do not pride themselves on their good observance; but, convinced that the good which is in them cannot come from themselves and must be from the Lord, glorify the Lord's work in them, using the words of the Prophet, "Not to us, O Lord, not to us, but to Your name give the glory." Thus also the Apostle Paul attributed nothing of the success of his preaching to himself, but said, "By the grace of God I am what I am." And again he says, "He who glories, let him glory in the Lord."

Jan. 5—May 6—Sept. 5

Hence the Lord says in the Gospel, "Whoever listens to these words of Mine and acts upon them, I will liken him to a wise man who built his house on rock. The floods came, the winds blew and beat against that house, and it did not fall, because it was founded on rock."

Having given us these assurances, the Lord is waiting every day for us to respond by our deeds to His holy admonitions. And the days of this life are lengthened and a truce granted us for this very reason, that we may amend our evil ways. As the Apostle says, "Do you not know that God's patience is inviting you to repent?" For the merciful Lord tells us, "I desire not the death of the sinner, but that he should be converted and live."

Jan. 6—May 7—Sept. 6

So, brethren, we have asked the Lord who is to dwell in His tent, and we have heard His commands to anyone who would dwell there; it remains for us to fulfil those duties.

Therefore we must prepare our hearts and our bodies to do battle under the holy obedience of His commands; and let us ask God that He be pleased to give us the help of His grace for anything which our nature finds hardly possible. And if we want to escape the pains of hell and attain life everlasting, then, while there is still time, while we are still in the body and are able to fulfil all these things by the light of this life, we must hasten to do now what will profit us for eternity.

Jan. 7—May 8—Sept. 7

And so we are going to establish a school for the service of the Lord.

In founding it we hope to introduce nothing harsh or burdensome. But if a certain strictness results from the dictates of equity for the amendment of vices or the preservation of charity, do not be at once dismayed and fly from the way of salvation, whose entrance cannot but be narrow. For as we advance in the religious life and in faith, our hearts expand and we run the way of God's commandments with unspeakable sweetness of love. Thus, never departing from His school, but persevering in the monastery according to His teaching until death, we may by patience share in the sufferings of Christ and deserve to have a share also in His kingdom.

CHAPTER I
ON THE KINDS OF MONKS

Jan. 8—May 9—Sept. 8

It is well known that there are four kinds of monks. The first kind are the Cenobites: those who live in monasteries and serve under a rule and an Abbot.

The second kind are the Anchorites or Hermits: those who, no longer in the first fervor of their reformation, but after long probation in a monastery, having learned by the help of many brethren how to fight against the devil, go out well armed from the ranks of the community to the solitary combat of the desert. They are able now, with no help save from God, to fight single-handed against the vices of the flesh and their own evil thoughts.

The third kind of monks, a detestable kind, are the Sarabaites. These, not having been tested, as gold in the furnace, by any rule or by the lessons of experience, are as soft as lead. In their works they still keep faith with the world, so that their tonsure marks them as liars before God. They live in twos or threes, or even singly, without a shepherd, in their own sheepfolds and not in the Lord's. Their law is the desire for self-gratification: whatever enters their mind or appeals to them, that they call holy; what they dislike, they regard as unlawful.

The fourth kind of monks are those called Gyrovagues. These spend their whole lives tramping from province to province, staying as guests in different monasteries for three or four days at a time. Always on the move, with no stability, they indulge their own wills and succumb to the allurements of gluttony, and are in every way worse than the Sarabaites. Of the miserable conduct of all such men it is better to be silent than to speak.

Passing these over, therefore, let us proceed, with God's help, to lay down a rule for the strongest kind of monks, the Cenobites.

CHAPTER 2

WHAT KIND OF MAN THE ABBOT OUGHT TO BE

Jan. 9—May 10—Sept. 9

An Abbot who is worthy to be over a monastery should always remember what he is called, and live up to the name of Superior. For he is believed to hold the place of Christ in the monastery, being called by a name of His, which is taken from the words of the Apostle: "You have received a Spirit of adoption as sons, by virtue of which we cry, 'Abba—Father!'"

Therefore the Abbot ought not to teach or ordain or command anything which is against the Lord's precepts; on the contrary, his commands and his teaching should be a leaven of divine justice kneaded into the minds of his disciples.

Jan. 10—May 11—Sept. 10

Let the Abbot always bear in mind that at
the dread Judgment of God there will be an
examination of these two matters: his teaching
and the obedience of his disciples. And let the
Abbot be sure that any lack of profit the master of
the house may find in the sheep will be laid to the
blame of the shepherd. On the other hand, if the
shepherd has bestowed all his pastoral diligence
on a restless, unruly flock and tried every remedy
for their unhealthy behavior, then he will be
acquitted at the Lord's Judgment and may say to
the Lord with the Prophet: "I have not concealed
Your justice within my heart; Your truth and Your
salvation I have declared. But they have despised
and rejected me." And then finally let death itself,
irresistible, punish those disobedient sheep under
his charge.

Jan. 11—May 12—Sept. 11

Therefore, when anyone receives the name of
Abbot, he ought to govern his disciples with a
twofold teaching. That is to say, he should show
them all that is good and holy by his deeds even
more than by his words, expounding the Lord's

commandments in words to the intelligent among his disciples, but demonstrating the divine precepts by his actions for those of harder hearts and ruder minds. And whatever he has taught his disciples to be contrary to God's law, let him indicate by his example that it is not to be done, lest, while preaching to others, he himself be found reprobate, and lest God one day say to him in his sin, "Why do you declare My statutes and profess My covenant with your lips, whereas you hate discipline and have cast My words behind you?" And again, "You were looking at the speck in your brother's eye, and did not see the beam in your own."

Jan. 12—May 13—Sept. 12

Let him make no distinction of persons in the monastery. Let him not love one more than another, unless it be one whom he finds better in good works or in obedience. Let him not advance one of noble birth ahead of one who was formerly a slave, unless there be some other reasonable ground for it. But if the Abbot for just reason think fit to do so, let him advance one of any rank whatever. Otherwise let them keep their due places; because, whether slaves or freemen, we are all one in Christ and bear an equal burden of service in the army of the same Lord. For with God there is no respect of persons. Only for one reason are we preferred in His sight: if we be found better than others in good works and humility. Therefore let the Abbot show equal love to all and impose the same discipline on all according to their deserts.

Jan. 13—May 14—Sept. 13

In his teaching the Abbot should always follow the Apostle's formula: "Reprove, entreat, rebuke"; threatening at one time and coaxing at another as the occasion may require, showing now the stern countenance of a master, now the loving affection of a father. That is to say, it is the undisciplined and restless whom he must reprove rather sharply; it is the obedient, meek and patient whom he must entreat to advance in virtue; while as for the negligent and disdainful, these we charge him to rebuke and correct.

And let him not shut his eyes to the faults of offenders; but, since he has the authority, let him cut out those faults by the roots as soon as they begin to appear, remembering the fate of Heli, the priest of Silo. The well-disposed and those of good understanding let him correct with verbal admonition the first and second time. But bold, hard, proud and disobedient characters he should curb at the very beginning of their ill-doing by stripes and other bodily punishments, knowing that it is written, "The fool is not corrected with words," and again, "Beat your son with the rod and you will deliver his soul from death."

Jan. 14—May 15—Sept. 14

The Abbot should always remember what he is and what he is called, and should know that to whom more is committed, from him more is required. Let him understand also what a difficult and arduous task he has undertaken: ruling souls and adapting himself to a variety of characters. One he must coax, another scold, another persuade, according to each one's character and understanding. Thus he must adjust and adapt himself to all in such a way that he may not only suffer no loss in the flock committed to his care, but may even rejoice in the increase of a good flock.

Jan. 15—May 16—Sept. 15

Above all let him not neglect or undervalue the welfare of the souls committed to him, in a greater concern for fleeting, earthly, perishable things; but let him always bear in mind that he has undertaken the government of souls and that he will have to give an account of them.

And if he be tempted to allege a lack of earthly means, let him remember what is written: "First seek the kingdom of God and His justice, and all these things shall be given you besides." And again: "Nothing is wanting to those who fear Him."

Let him know, then, that he who has undertaken the government of souls must prepare himself to render an account of them. Whatever number of brethren he knows he has under his care, he may be sure beyond doubt that on Judgment Day he will have to give the Lord an account of all these souls, as well as of his own soul.

Thus the constant apprehension about his coming examination as shepherd concerning the sheep entrusted to him, and his anxiety over the account that must be given for others, make him careful of his own record. And while by his admonitions he is helping others to amend, he himself is cleansed of his faults.

CHAPTER 3

ON CALLING THE BRETHREN FOR COUNSEL

Jan. 16—May 17—Sept. 16

Whenever any important business has to be done in the monastery, let the Abbot call together the whole community and state the matter to be acted upon. Then, having heard the brethren's advice, let him turn the matter over in his own mind and do what he shall judge to be most expedient.

The reason we have said that all should be called for counsel is that the Lord often reveals to the younger what is best.

Let the brethren give their advice with all the deference required by humility, and not presume stubbornly to defend their opinions; but let the decision rather depend on the Abbot's judgment, and all submit to whatever he shall decide for their welfare.

However, just as it is proper for the disciples to obey their master, so also it is his function to dispose all things with prudence and justice.

Jan. 17—May 18—Sept. 17

In all things, therefore, let all follow the Rule as guide, and let no one be so rash as to deviate from it. Let no one in the monastery follow his own heart's fancy; and let no one presume to contend with his Abbot in an insolent way or even outside of the monastery. But if anyone should presume to do so, let him undergo the discipline of the Rule. At the same time, the Abbot himself should do all things in the fear of God and in observance of the Rule, knowing that beyond a doubt he will have to render an account of all his decisions to God, the most just Judge.

But if the business to be done in the interests of the monastery be of lesser importance, let him take counsel with the seniors only. It is written, "Do everything with counsel, and you will not repent when you have done it."

CHAPTER 4

WHAT ARE THE INSTRUMENTS OF GOOD WORKS

Jan. 18—May 19—Sept. 18

1. In the first place, to love the Lord God with the whole heart, the whole soul, the whole strength.
2. Then, one's neighbor as oneself.
3. Then not to murder.
4. Not to commit adultery.
5. Not to steal.
6. Not to covet.
7. Not to bear false witness.
8. To respect all men.
9. And not to do to another what one would not have done to oneself.

10. To deny oneself in order to follow Christ.
11. To chastise the body.
12. Not to become attached to pleasures.
13. To love fasting.
14. To relieve the poor.
15. To clothe the naked.
16. To visit the sick.
17. To bury the dead.
18. To help in trouble.
19. To console the sorrowing.
20. To become a stranger to the world's ways.
21. To prefer nothing to the love of Christ.

Jan. 19—May 20—Sept. 19

22. Not to give way to anger.
23. Not to nurse a grudge.
24. Not to entertain deceit in one's heart.
25. Not to give a false peace.
26. Not to forsake charity.
27. Not to swear, for fear of perjuring oneself.
28. To utter truth from heart and mouth.
29. Not to return evil for evil.
30. To do no wrong to anyone, and to bear patiently wrongs done to oneself.
31. To love one's enemies.

32. Not to curse those who curse us, but rather to bless them.
33. To bear persecution for justice's sake.
34. Not to be proud.
35. Not addicted to wine.
36. Not a great eater.
37. Not drowsy.
38. Not lazy.
39. Not a grumbler.
40. Not a detractor.
41. To put one's hope in God.
42. To attribute to God, and not to self, whatever good one sees in oneself.
43. But to recognize always that the evil is one's own doing, and to impute it to oneself.

Jan. 20—May 21—Sept. 20

44. To fear the Day of Judgment.
45. To be in dread of hell.
46. To desire eternal life with all the passion of the spirit.
47. To keep death daily before one's eyes.
48. To keep constant guard over the actions of one's life.

49. To know for certain that God sees one everywhere.
50. When evil thoughts come into one's heart, to dash them against Christ immediately.
51. And to manifest them to one's spiritual father.
52. To guard one's tongue against evil and depraved speech.
53. Not to love much talking.
54. Not to speak useless words or words that move to laughter.
55. Not to love much or boisterous laughter.
56. To listen willingly to holy reading.
57. To devote oneself frequently to prayer.
58. Daily in one's prayers, with tears and sighs, to confess one's past sins to God, and to amend them for the future.
59. Not to fulfil the desires of the flesh; to hate one's own will.
60. To obey in all things the commands of the Abbot, even though he himself (which God forbid) should act otherwise, mindful of the Lord's precept, "Do what they say, but not what they do."
61. Not to wish to be called holy before one is holy; but first to be holy, that one may be truly so called.

Jan. 21—May 22—Sept. 21

62. To fulfil God's commandments daily in one's deeds.
63. To love chastity.
64. To hate no one.
65. Not to be jealous, not to harbor envy.
66. Not to love contention.
67. To beware of haughtiness.
68. And to respect the seniors.
69. To love the juniors.
70. To pray for one's enemies in the love of Christ.
71. To make peace with one's adversary before the sun sets.
72. And never to despair of God's mercy.

These, then, are the tools of the spiritual craft. If we employ them unceasingly day and night, and return them on the Day of Judgment, our compensation from the Lord will be that wage He has promised: "Eye has not seen, nor ear heard, what God has prepared for those who love Him."

Now the workshop in which we shall diligently execute all these tasks is the enclosure of the monastery and stability in the community.

CHAPTER 5

ON OBEDIENCE

Jan. 22—May 23—Sept. 22

The first degree of humility is obedience without delay. This is the virtue of those who hold nothing dearer to them than Christ; who, because of the holy service they have professed, and the fear of hell, and the glory of life everlasting, as soon as anything has been ordered by the Superior, receive it as a divine command and cannot suffer any delay in executing it. Of these the Lord says, "As soon as he heard, he obeyed Me." And again to teachers He says, "He who hears you, hears Me."

Such as these, therefore, immediately leaving their own affairs and forsaking their own will, dropping the work they were engaged in and leaving it unfinished, with the ready step of obedience follow up with their deeds the voice of him who commands. And so as it were at the same moment the master's command is given and the disciple's work is completed, the two things being speedily accomplished together in the swiftness of the fear of God by those who are moved with the desire of attaining life everlasting. That desire is their motive for choosing the narrow way, of which the Lord says, "Narrow is the way that leads to life," so that, not living according to their own choice nor obeying their own desires and pleasures but walking by another's judgment and command, they dwell in monasteries and desire to have an Abbot over them. Assuredly such as these are living up to that maxim of the Lord in which He says, "I have come not to do My own will, but the will of Him who sent Me."

Jan. 23—May 24—Sept. 23

But this very obedience will be acceptable to God and pleasing to men only if what is commanded is done without hesitation, delay, lukewarmness, grumbling, or objection. For the obedience given to Superiors is given to God, since He Himself has said, "He who hears you, hears Me." And the disciples should offer their obedience with a good will, for "God loves a cheerful giver." For if the disciple obeys with an ill will and murmurs, not necessarily with his lips but simply in his heart, then even though he fulfil the command yet his work will not be acceptable to God, who sees that his heart is murmuring. And, far from gaining a reward for such work as this, he will incur the punishment due to murmurers, unless he amend and make satisfaction.

CHAPTER 6

ON THE SPIRIT OF SILENCE

Jan. 24—May 25—Sept. 24

Let us do what the Prophet says: "I said, 'I will guard my ways, that I may not sin with my tongue. I have set a guard to my mouth.' I was mute and was humbled, and kept silence even from good things." Here the Prophet shows that if the spirit of silence ought to lead us at times to refrain even from good speech, so much the more ought the punishment for sin make us avoid evil words.

Therefore, since the spirit of silence is so important, permission to speak should rarely be granted even to perfect disciples, even though it be for good, holy, edifying conversation; for it is written, "In much speaking you will not escape sin," and in another place, "Death and life are in the power of the tongue."

For speaking and teaching belong to the master; the disciple's part is to be silent and to listen. And for that reason if anything has to be asked of the Superior, it should be asked with all the humility and submission inspired by reverence.

But as for coarse jests and idle words or words that move to laughter, these we condemn everywhere with a perpetual ban, and for such conversation we do not permit a disciple to open his mouth.

CHAPTER 7
ON HUMILITY

Jan. 25—May 26—Sept. 25

Holy Scripture, brethren, cries out to us, saying, "Everyone who exalts himself shall be humbled, and he who humbles himself shall be exalted." In saying this it shows us that all exaltation is a kind of pride, against which the Prophet proves himself to be on guard when he says, "Lord, my heart is not exalted, nor are mine eyes lifted up; neither have I walked in great matters, nor in wonders above me." But how has he acted? "Rather have I been of humble mind than exalting myself; as a weaned child on its mother's breast, so You solace my soul."

Hence, brethren, if we wish to reach the very highest point of humility and to arrive speedily at that heavenly exaltation to which ascent is made through the humility of this present life, we must by our ascending actions erect the ladder Jacob saw in his dream, on which Angels appeared to him descending and ascending. By that descent and ascent we must surely understand nothing else than this, that we descend by self-exaltation and ascend by humility. And the ladder thus set up is our life in the world, which the Lord raises up to heaven if our heart is humbled. For we call our body and soul the sides of the ladder, and into these sides our divine vocation has inserted the different steps of humility and discipline we must climb.

Jan. 26—May 27—Sept. 26

The first degree of humility, then, is that a person keep the fear of God before his eyes and beware of ever forgetting it. Let him be ever mindful of all that God has commanded; let his thoughts constantly recur to the hell-fire which will burn for their sins those who despise God, and to the life everlasting which is prepared for those who fear Him.

Let him keep himself at every moment from sins and vices, whether of the mind, the tongue, the hands, the feet, or the self-will, and check also the desires of the flesh.

Jan. 27—May 28—Sept. 27

Let a man consider that God is always looking at him from heaven, that his actions are everywhere visible to the divine eyes and are constantly being reported to God by the Angels. This is what the Prophet shows us when he represents God as ever present within our thoughts, in the words "Searcher of minds and hearts is God" and again in the words "The Lord knows the thoughts of men." Again he says, "You have read my thoughts from afar" and "The thoughts of men will confess to You."

In order that he may be careful about his wrongful thoughts, therefore, let the faithful brother say constantly in his heart, "Then shall I be spotless before Him, if I have kept myself from my iniquity."

Jan. 28—May 29—Sept. 28

As for self-will, we are forbidden to do our own will by the Scripture, which says to us, "Turn away from your own will," and likewise by the prayer in which we ask God that His will be done in us. And rightly are we taught not to do our own will when we take heed to the warning of Scripture: "There are ways which to men seem right, but the ends of them plunge into the depths of hell"; and also when we tremble at what is said of the careless: "They are corrupt and have become abominable in their wills."

And as for the desires of the flesh, let us believe with the Prophet that God is ever present to us, when he says to the Lord, "Every desire of mine is before You."

Jan. 29—May 30—Sept. 29

We must be on our guard, therefore, against evil desires, for death lies close by the gate of pleasure. Hence the Scripture gives this command: "Go not after your concupiscences."

So therefore, since the eyes of the Lord observe the good and the evil and the Lord is always looking down from heaven on the children of men "to see if there be anyone who understands and seeks God," and since our deeds are daily, day and night, reported to the Lord by the Angels assigned to us, we must constantly beware, brethren, as the Prophet says in the Psalm, lest at any time God see us falling into evil ways and becoming unprofitable; and lest, having spared us for the present because in His kindness He awaits our reformation, He say to us in the future, "These things you did, and I held My peace."

Jan. 30—May 31—Sept. 30

The second degree of humility is that a person love not his own will nor take pleasure in satisfying his desires, but model his actions on the saying of the Lord, "I have come not to do My own will, but the will of Him who sent Me." It is written also, "Self-will has its punishment, but constraint wins a crown."

Jan. 31—June 1—Oct. 1

The third degree of humility is that a person for love of God submit himself to his Superior in all obedience, imitating the Lord, of whom the Apostle says, "He became obedient even unto death."

Feb. 1—June 2—Oct. 2

The fourth degree of humility is that he hold fast to patience with a silent mind when in this obedience he meets with difficulties and contradictions and even any kind of injustice, enduring all without growing weary or running away. For the Scripture says, "He who perseveres to the end, he it is who shall be saved"; and again, "Let your heart take courage, and wait for the Lord!"

And to show how those who are faithful ought to endure all things, however contrary, for the Lord, the Scripture says in the person of the suffering, "For Your sake we are put to death all the day long; we are considered as sheep marked for slaughter." Then, secure in their hope of a divine recompense, they go on with joy to declare, "But in all these trials we conquer, through Him who has granted us His love." Again, in another place the Scripture says, "You have tested us, O God; You have tried us as silver is tried, by fire; You have brought us into a snare; You have laid afflictions on our back." And to show that we ought to be under a Superior, it goes on to say, "You have set men over our heads."

Moreover, by their patience those faithful ones fulfil the Lord's command in adversities and injuries: when struck on one cheek, they offer the other; when deprived of their tunic, they surrender also their cloak; when forced to go a mile, they go two; with the Apostle Paul they bear with false brethren and bless those who curse them.

Feb. 2—June 3—Oct. 3

The fifth degree of humility is that he hide from his Abbot none of the evil thoughts that enter his heart or the sins committed in secret, but that he humbly confess them. The Scripture urges us to this when it says, "Reveal your way to the Lord and hope in Him," and again, "Confess to the Lord, for He is good, for His mercy endures forever." And the Prophet likewise says, "My offence I have made known to You, and my iniquities I have not covered up. I said: 'I will declare against myself my iniquities to the Lord'; and 'You forgave the wickedness of my heart.'"

Feb. 3—June 4—Oct. 4

The sixth degree of humility is that a monk be content with the poorest and worst of everything, and that in every occupation assigned him he consider himself a bad and worthless workman, saying with the Prophet, "I am brought to nothing and I am without understanding; I have become as a beast of burden before You, and I am always with You."

Feb. 4—June 5—Oct. 5

The seventh degree of humility is that he consider himself lower and of less account than anyone else, and this not only in verbal protestation but also with the most heartfelt inner conviction, humbling himself and saying with the Prophet, "But I am a worm and no man, the scorn of men and the outcast of the people. After being exalted, I have been humbled and covered with confusion." And again, "It is good for me that You have humbled me, that I may learn Your commandments."

Feb. 5—June 6—Oct. 6

The eighth degree of humility is that a monk do nothing except what is commended by the common Rule of the monastery and the example of the elders.

Feb. 6—June 7—Oct. 7

The ninth degree of humility is that a monk restrain his tongue and keep silence, not speaking until he is questioned. For the Scripture shows that "in much speaking there is no escape from sin" and that "the talkative man is not stable on the earth."

Feb. 7—June 8—Oct. 8

The tenth degree of humility is that he be not ready and quick to laugh, for it is written, "The fool lifts up his voice in laughter."

Feb. 8—June 9—Oct. 9

The eleventh degree of humility is that when a monk speaks he do so gently and without laughter, humbly and seriously, in few and sensible words, and that he be not noisy in his speech. It is written, "A wise man is known by the fewness of his words."

Feb. 9—June 10—Oct. 10

The twelfth degree of humility is that a monk not only have humility in his heart but also by his very appearance make it always manifest to those who see him. That is to say that whether he is at the Work of God, in the oratory, in the monastery, in the garden, on the road, in the fields or anywhere else, and whether sitting, walking or standing, he should always have his head bowed and his eyes toward the ground. Feeling the guilt of his sins at every moment, he should consider himself already present at the dread Judgment and constantly say in his heart what the publican in the Gospel said with his eyes fixed on the earth: "Lord, I am a sinner and not worthy to lift up my eyes to heaven"; and again with the Prophet: "I am bowed down and humbled everywhere." Having climbed all these steps of humility, therefore, the monk will presently come to that perfect love of God which casts out fear. And all those precepts which formerly he had not observed without fear, he will now begin to keep by reason of that love, without any effort, as though naturally and by habit. No longer will his motive be the fear of hell, but rather the love of Christ, good habit and delight in the virtues which the Lord will deign to show forth by the Holy Spirit in His servant now cleansed from vice and sin.

CHAPTER 8

ON THE DIVINE OFFICE DURING THE NIGHT

Feb. 10—June 11—Oct. 11

In winter time, that is from the Calends of November until Easter, the brethren shall rise at what is calculated to be the eighth hour of the night, so that they may sleep somewhat longer than half the night and rise with their rest completed. And the time that remains after the Night Office should be spent in study by those brethren who need a better knowledge of the Psalter or the lessons.

From Easter to the aforesaid Calends of November, the hour of rising should be so arranged that the Morning Office, which is to be said at daybreak, will follow the Night Office after a very short interval, during which the brethren may go out for the necessities of nature.

CHAPTER 9

HOW MANY PSALMS ARE TO BE SAID AT THE NIGHT OFFICE

Feb. 11—June 12—Oct. 12

In winter time as defined above, there is first this verse to be said three times: "O Lord, open my lips, and my mouth shall declare Your praise." To it is added Psalm 3 and the "Glory be to the Father," and after that Psalm 94 to be chanted with an antiphon or even chanted simply. Let the Ambrosian hymn follow next, and then six Psalms with antiphons. When these are finished and the verse said, let the Abbot give a blessing; then, all being seated on the benches, let three lessons be read from the book on the lectern by the brethren in their turns, and after each lesson let a responsory be chanted. Two of the responsories are to be said without a "Glory be to the Father"; but after the third lesson let the chanter say the "Glory be to the Father," and as soon as he begins it let all rise from their seats out of honor and reverence to the Holy Trinity.

The books to be read at the Night Office shall be those of divine authorship, of both the Old and the New Testament, and also the explanations of them which have been made by well known and orthodox Catholic Fathers.

After these three lessons with their responsories let the remaining six Psalms follow, to be chanted with "Alleluia." After these shall follow the lesson from the Apostle, to be recited by heart, the verse and the petition of the litany, that is "Lord, have mercy on us." And so let the Night Office come to an end.

CHAPTER 10

HOW THE NIGHT OFFICE IS TO BE SAID IN SUMMER TIME

Feb. 12—June 13—Oct. 13

From Easter until the Calends of November let the same number of Psalms be kept as prescribed above; but no lessons are to be read from the book, on account of the shortness of the nights. Instead of those three lessons let one lesson from the Old Testament be said by heart and followed by a short responsory. But all the rest should be done as has been said, that is to say that never fewer than twelve Psalms should be said at the Night Office, not counting Psalm 3 and Psalm 94.

CHAPTER II

HOW THE NIGHT OFFICE IS TO BE SAID ON SUNDAYS

Feb. 13—June 14—Oct. 14

On Sunday the hour of rising for the Night Office should be earlier. In that Office let the measure already prescribed be kept, namely the singing of six Psalms and a verse. Then let all be seated on the benches in their proper order while the lessons and their responsories are read from the book, as we said above. These shall be four in number, with the chanter saying the "Glory be to the Father" in the fourth responsory only, and all rising reverently as soon as he begins it.

After these lessons let six more Psalms with antiphons follow in order, as before, and a verse;

and then let four more lessons be read with their responsories in the same way as the former.

After these let there be three canticles from the book of the Prophets, as the Abbot shall appoint, and let these canticles be chanted with "Alleluia." Then when the verse has been said and the Abbot has given the blessing, let four more lessons be read, from the New Testament, in the manner prescribed above.

After the fourth responsory let the Abbot begin the hymn "We praise You, O God." When this is finished the Abbot shall read the lesson from the book of the Gospels, while all stand in reverence and awe. At the end let all answer "Amen," and let the Abbot proceed at once to the hymn "To You be praise." After the blessing has been given, let them begin the Morning Office.

This order for the Night Office on Sunday shall be observed the year around, both summer and winter; unless it should happen (which God forbid) that the brethren be late in rising, in which case the lessons or the responsories will have to be shortened somewhat. Let every precaution be taken, however, against such an occurrence; but if it does happen, then the one through whose neglect it has come about should make due satisfaction to God in the oratory.

CHAPTER 12

HOW THE MORNING OFFICE IS TO BE SAID

Feb. 14—June 15—Oct. 15

The Morning Office on Sunday shall begin with Psalm 66 recited straight through without an antiphon. After that let Psalm 50 be said with "Alleluia," then Psalms 117 and 62, the Canticle of Blessing and the Psalms of praise; then a lesson from the Apocalypse to be recited by heart, the responsory, the Ambrosian hymn, the verse, the canticle from the Gospel book, the litany and so the end.

CHAPTER 13

HOW THE MORNING OFFICE IS TO BE SAID ON WEEKDAYS

Feb. 15—June 16—Oct. 16

On weekdays the Morning Office shall be celebrated as follows. Let Psalm 66 be said without an antiphon and somewhat slowly, as on Sunday, in order that all may be in time for Psalm 50, which is to be said with an antiphon. After that let two other Psalms be said according to custom, namely: on Monday Psalms 5 and 35, on Tuesday Psalms 42 and 56, on Wednesday Psalms 63 and 64, on Thursday Psalms 87 and 89, on Friday Psalms 75 and 91, and on Saturday Psalm 142 and the canticle from Deuteronomy, which is to be divided into two sections each terminated by a

"Glory be to the Father." But on the other days let there be a canticle from the Prophets, each on its own day as chanted by the Roman Church. Next follow the Psalms of praise, then a lesson of the Apostle to be recited from memory, the responsory, the Ambrosian hymn, the verse, the canticle from the Gospel book, the litany, and so the end.

Feb. 16—June 17—Oct. 17

The Morning and Evening Offices should never be allowed to pass without the Superior saying the Lord's Prayer in its place at the end so that all may hear it, on account of the thorns of scandal which are apt to spring up. Thus those who hear it, being warned by the covenant which they make in that prayer when they say, "Forgive us as we forgive," may cleanse themselves of faults against that covenant.

But at the other Offices let the last part only of that prayer be said aloud, so that all may answer, "But deliver us from evil."

CHAPTER 14

HOW THE NIGHT OFFICE IS TO BE SAID ON THE FEASTS OF THE SAINTS

Feb. 17—June 18—Oct. 18

On the feasts of Saints and on all festivals let the Office be performed as we have prescribed for Sundays, except that the Psalms, the antiphons and the lessons belonging to that particular day are to be said. Their number, however, shall remain as we have specified above.

CHAPTER 15

AT WHAT TIMES "ALLELUIA" IS TO BE SAID

Feb. 18—June 19—Oct. 19

From holy Easter until Pentecost without interruption let "Alleluia" be said both in the Psalms and in the responsories. From Pentecost to the beginning of Lent let it be said every night with the last six Psalms of the Night Office only. On every Sunday, however, outside of Lent, the canticles, the Morning Office, Prime, Terce, Sext and None shall be said with "Alleluia," but Vespers with antiphons.

The responsories are never to be said with "Alleluia" except from Easter to Pentecost.

CHAPTER 16

HOW THE WORK OF GOD IS TO BE PERFORMED DURING THE DAY

Feb. 19—June 20—Oct. 20

"Seven times in the day," says the Prophet, "I have rendered praise to You." Now that sacred number of seven will be fulfilled by us if we perform the Offices of our service at the time of the Morning Office, of Prime, of Terce, of Sext, of None, of Vespers and of Compline, since it was of these day Hours that he said, "Seven times in the day I have rendered praise to You." For as to the Night Office the same Prophet says, "In the middle of the night I arose to glorify You."

Let us therefore bring our tribute of praise to our Creator "for the judgments of His justice" at these times: the Morning Office, Prime, Terce, Sext, None, Vespers and Compline; and in the night let us arise to glorify Him.

CHAPTER 17

HOW MANY PSALMS ARE TO BE SAID AT THESE HOURS

Feb. 20—June 21—Oct. 21

We have already arranged the order of the psalmody for the Night and Morning Offices; let us now provide for the remaining Hours.

At Prime let three Psalms be said, separately and not under one "Glory be to the Father." The hymn of that Hour is to follow the verse "Incline unto my aid, O God," before the Psalms begin. Upon completion of the three Psalms let one lesson be recited, then a verse, the "Lord, have mercy on us" and the concluding prayers.

The Offices of Terce, Sext and None are to be celebrated in the same order, that is: the "Incline unto my aid, O God," the hymn proper to each Hour, three Psalms, lesson and verse, "Lord, have mercy on us" and concluding prayers.

If the community is a large one, let the Psalms be sung with antiphons; but if small, let them be sung straight through.

Let the Psalms of the Vesper Office be limited to four, with antiphons. After these Psalms the lesson is to be recited, then the responsory, the Ambrosian hymn, the verse, the canticle from the Gospel book, the litany, the Lord's Prayer and the concluding prayers.

Let Compline be limited to the saying of three Psalms, which are to be said straight through without antiphon, and after them the hymn of that Hour, one lesson, a verse, the "Lord, have mercy on us," the blessing and the concluding prayers.

CHAPTER 18

IN WHAT ORDER THE PSALMS ARE TO BE SAID

Feb. 21—June 22—Oct. 22

Let this verse be said: "Incline unto my aid, O God; O Lord, make haste to help me," and the "Glory be to the Father"; then the hymn proper to each Hour.

Then at Prime on Sunday four sections of Psalm 118 are to be said; and at each of the remaining Hours, that is Terce, Sext and None, three sections of the same Psalm 118.

At Prime on Monday let three Psalms be said, namely Psalms 1, 2 and 6. And so each day at Prime until Sunday let three Psalms be said in numerical order, to Psalm 19, but with Psalms 9 and 17 each divided into two parts. Thus it comes about that the Night Office on Sunday always begins with Psalm 20.

Feb. 22—June 23—Oct. 23

At Terce, Sext and None on Monday let the nine remaining sections of Psalm 118 be said, three at each of these Hours.

Psalm 118 having been completed, therefore, on two days, Sunday and Monday, let the nine Psalms from Psalm 119 to Psalm 127 be said at Terce, Sext and None, three at each Hour, beginning with Tuesday. And let these same Psalms be repeated every day until Sunday at the same Hours, while the arrangement of hymns, lessons and verses is kept the same on all days; and thus Prime on Sunday will always begin with Psalm 118.

Feb. 23—June 24—Oct. 24

Vespers are to be sung with four Psalms every day. These shall begin with Psalm 109 and go on to Psalm 147, omitting those which are set apart for other Hours; that is to say that with the exception of Psalms 117 to 127 and Psalms 133 and 142, all the rest of these are to be said at Vespers. And since there are three Psalms too few, let the longer ones of the above number be divided, namely Psalms

138, 143 and 144. But let Psalm 116 because of its brevity be joined to Psalm 115.

The order of the Vesper Psalms being thus settled, let the rest of the Hour—lesson, responsory, hymn, verse and canticle—be carried out as we prescribed above.

At Compline the same Psalms are to be repeated every day, namely Psalms 4, 90 and 133.

(Feb. 24 in leap year; otherwise added to the preceding)—June 25—Oct. 25

The order of psalmody for the day Hours being thus arranged, let all the remaining Psalms be equally distributed among the seven Night Offices by dividing the longer Psalms among them and assigning twelve Psalms to each night.

We strongly recommend, however, that if this distribution of the Psalms is displeasing to anyone, he should arrange them otherwise, in whatever way he considers better, but taking care in any case that the Psalter with its full number of 150 Psalms be chanted every week and begun again every Sunday at the Night Office. For those monks show themselves too lazy in the service to which they are vowed, who chant less than the Psalter with the customary canticles in the course of a week, whereas we read that our holy Fathers strenuously fulfilled that task in a single day. May we, lukewarm that we are, perform it at least in a whole week!

CHAPTER 19

ON THE MANNER OF SAYING THE DIVINE OFFICE

Feb. 24 (25)—June 26—Oct. 26

We believe that the divine presence is everywhere and that "the eyes of the Lord are looking on the good and the evil in every place." But we should believe this especially without any doubt when we are assisting at the Work of God. To that end let us be mindful always of the Prophet's words, "Serve the Lord in fear," and again "Sing praises wisely," and "In the sight of the Angels I will sing praise to You." Let us therefore consider how we ought to conduct ourselves in the sight of the Godhead and of His Angels, and let us take part in the psalmody in such a way that our mind may be in harmony with our voice.

CHAPTER 20

ON REVERENCE IN PRAYER

Feb. 25 (26)—June 27—Oct. 27

When we wish to suggest our wants to men of high station, we do not presume to do so except with humility and reverence. How much the more, then, are complete humility and pure devotion necessary in supplication of the Lord who is God of the universe! And let us be assured that it is not in saying a great deal that we shall be heard, but in purity of heart and in tears of compunction. Our prayer, therefore, ought to be short and pure, unless it happens to be prolonged by an inspiration of divine grace. In community, however, let prayer be very short, and when the Superior gives the signal let all rise together.

CHAPTER 21

ON THE DEANS OF THE MONASTERY

Feb. 26 (27)—June 28—Oct. 28

If the community is a large one, let there be chosen out of it brethren of good repute and holy life, and let them be appointed deans. These shall take charge of their deaneries in all things, observing the commandments of God and the instructions of their Abbot.

Let men of such character be chosen deans that the Abbot may with confidence share his burdens among them. Let them be chosen not by rank but according to their worthiness of life and the wisdom of their doctrine.

If any of these deans should become inflated with pride and found deserving of censure, let him be corrected once, and again, and a third time. If he will not amend, then let him be deposed and another be put in his place who is worthy of it.

And we order the same to be done in the case of the Prior.

CHAPTER 22

HOW THE MONKS ARE TO SLEEP

Feb. 27 (28)—June 29—Oct. 29

Let each one sleep in a separate bed. Let them receive bedding suitable to their manner of life, according to the Abbot's directions. If possible let all sleep in one place; but if the number does not allow this, let them take their rest by tens or twenties with the seniors who have charge of them.

A candle shall be kept burning in the room until morning.

Let the monks sleep clothed and girded with belts or cords—but not with their knives at their sides, lest they cut themselves in their sleep—and thus be always ready to rise without delay when the signal is given and hasten to be before one another at the Work of God, yet with all gravity and decorum.

The younger brethren shall not have beds next to one another, but among those of the older ones.

When they rise for the Work of God let them gently encourage one another, that the drowsy may have no excuse.

CHAPTER 23

ON EXCOMMUNICATION FOR FAULTS

Feb. 28 (29)—June 30—Oct. 30

If a brother is found to be obstinate, or disobedient, or proud, or murmuring, or habitually transgressing the Holy Rule in any point and contemptuous of the orders of his seniors, the latter shall admonish him secretly a first and a second time, as Our Lord commands. If he fails to amend, let him be given a public rebuke in front of the whole community. But if even then he does not reform, let him be placed under excommunication, provided that he understands the seriousness of that penalty; if he is perverse, however, let him undergo corporal punishment.

CHAPTER 24

WHAT THE MEASURE OF EXCOMMUNICATION SHOULD BE

Mar. 1—July 1—Oct. 31

The measure of excommunication or of chastisement should correspond to the degree of fault, which degree is estimated by the Abbot's judgment.

If a brother is found guilty of lighter faults, let him be excluded from the common table. Now the program for one deprived of the fellowship of the table shall be as follows: In the oratory he shall intone neither Psalm nor antiphon nor shall he recite a lesson until he has made satisfaction; in the refectory he shall take his food alone after the community meal, so that if the brethren eat at the sixth hour, for instance, that brother shall eat at the ninth, while if they eat at the ninth hour he shall eat in the evening, until by a suitable satisfaction he obtains pardon.

CHAPTER 25
ON WEIGHTIER FAULTS

Mar. 2—July 2—Nov. 1

Let the brother who is guilty of a weightier fault be excluded both from the table and from the oratory. Let none of the brethren join him either for company or for conversation. Let him be alone at the work assigned him, abiding in penitential sorrow and pondering that terrible sentence of the Apostle where he says that a man of that kind is handed over for the destruction of the flesh, that the spirit may be saved in the day of the Lord. Let him take his meals alone in the measure and at the hour which the Abbot shall consider suitable for him. He shall not be blessed by those who pass by, nor shall the food that is given him be blessed.

CHAPTER 26

ON THOSE WHO WITHOUT AN ORDER ASSOCIATE WITH THE EXCOMMUNICATED

Mar. 3—July 3—Nov. 2

If any brother presumes without an order from the Abbot to associate in any way with an excommunicated brother, or to speak with him, or to send him a message, let him incur a similar punishment of excommunication.

CHAPTER 27

HOW SOLICITOUS THE ABBOT SHOULD BE FOR THE EXCOMMUNICATED

Mar. 4—July 4—Nov. 3

Let the Abbot be most solicitous in his concern for delinquent brethren, for "it is not the healthy but the sick who need a physician." And therefore he ought to use every means that a wise physician would use.

Let him send "senpectae," that is, brethren of mature years and wisdom, who may as it were secretly console the wavering brother and induce him to make humble satisfaction; comforting him that he may not "be overwhelmed by excessive grief," but that, as the Apostle says, charity may be strengthened in him. And let everyone pray for him.

For the Abbot must have the utmost solicitude and exercise all prudence and diligence lest he lose any of the sheep entrusted to him. Let him know that what he has undertaken is the care of weak souls and not a tyranny over strong ones; and let him fear the Prophet's warning through which God says, "What you saw to be fat you took to yourselves, and what was feeble you cast away." Let him rather imitate the loving example of the Good Shepherd who left the ninety-nine sheep in the mountains and went to look for the one sheep that had gone astray, on whose weakness He had such compassion that He deigned to place it on His own sacred shoulders and thus carry it back to the flock.

CHAPTER 28

ON THOSE WHO WILL NOT AMEND AFTER REPEATED CORRECTIONS

Mar. 5—July 5—Nov. 4

If a brother who has been frequently corrected for some fault, and even excommunicated, does not amend, let a harsher correction be applied, that is, let the punishment of the rod be administered to him.

But if he still does not reform or perhaps (which God forbid) even rises up in pride and wants to defend his conduct, then let the Abbot do what a wise physician would do. Having used applications, the ointments of exhortation, the medicines of the Holy Scriptures, finally the cautery of excommunication and of the strokes of the rod, if he sees that his efforts are of no avail, let him apply a still greater remedy, his own prayers and those of all the brethren, that the Lord, who can do all things, may restore health to the sick brother.

But if he is not healed even in this way, then let the Abbot use the knife of amputation, according to the Apostle's words, "Expel the evil one from your midst," and again, "If the faithless one departs, let him depart," lest one diseased sheep contaminate the whole flock.

CHAPTER 29

WHETHER BRETHREN WHO LEAVE THE MONASTERY SHOULD BE RECEIVED AGAIN

Mar. 6—July 6—Nov. 5

If a brother who through his own fault leaves the monastery should wish to return, let him first promise full reparation for his having gone away; and then let him be received in the lowest place, as a test of his humility. And if he should leave again, let him be taken back again, and so a third time; but he should understand that after this all way of return is denied him.

CHAPTER 30

HOW BOYS ARE TO BE CORRECTED

Mar. 7—July 7—Nov. 6

Every age and degree of understanding should have its proper measure of discipline. With regard to boys and adolescents, therefore, or those who cannot understand the seriousness of the penalty of excommunication, whenever such as these are delinquent let them be subjected to severe fasts or brought to terms by harsh beatings, that they may be cured.

CHAPTER 31

WHAT KIND OF MAN THE CELLARER OF THE MONASTERY SHOULD BE

Mar. 8—July 8—Nov. 7

As cellarer of the monastery let there be chosen from the community one who is wise, of mature character, sober, not a great eater, not haughty, not excitable, not offensive, not slow, not wasteful, but a God-fearing man who may be like a father to the whole community.

Let him have charge of everything. He shall do nothing without the Abbot's orders, but keep to his instructions. Let him not vex the brethren. If any brother happens to make some unreasonable demand of him, instead of vexing the brother with a contemptuous refusal he should humbly give the reason for denying the improper request.

Let him keep guard over his own soul, mindful always of the Apostle's saying that "he who has ministered well acquires for himself a good standing."

Let him take the greatest care of the sick, of children, of guests and of the poor, knowing without doubt that he will have to render an account for all these on the Day of Judgment.

Let him regard all the utensils of the monastery and its whole property as if they were the sacred vessels of the altar. Let him not think that he may neglect anything. He should be neither a miser nor a prodigal and squanderer of the monastery's substance, but should do all things with measure and in accordance with the Abbot's instructions.

Mar. 9—July 9—Nov. 8

Above all things let him have humility; and if he has nothing else to give let him give a good word in answer, for it is written, "A good word is above the best gift."

Let him have under his care all that the Abbot has assigned to him, but not presume to deal with what he has forbidden him.

Let him give the brethren their appointed allowance of food without any arrogance or delay, that they may not be scandalized, mindful of the Word of God as to what he deserves "who shall scandalize one of the little ones."

If the community is a large one, let helpers be given him, that by their assistance he may fulfil with a quiet mind the office committed to him. The proper times should be observed in giving the things that have to be given and asking for the things that have to be asked for, that no one may be troubled or vexed in the house of God.

CHAPTER 32

ON THE TOOLS AND PROPERTY OF THE MONASTERY

Mar. 10—July 10—Nov. 9

For the care of the monastery's property in tools, clothing and other articles let the Abbot appoint brethren on whose manner of life and character he can rely; and let him, as he shall judge to be expedient, consign the various articles to them, to be looked after and to be collected again. The Abbot shall keep a list of these articles, so that as the brethren succeed one another in their assignments he may know what he gives and what he receives back.

If anyone treats the monastery's property in a slovenly or careless way, let him be corrected. If he fails to amend, let him undergo the discipline of the Rule.

CHAPTER 33

WHETHER MONKS OUGHT TO HAVE ANYTHING OF THEIR OWN

Mar. 11—July 11—Nov. 10

This vice especially is to be cut out of the monastery by the roots. Let no one presume to give or receive anything without the Abbot's leave, or to have anything as his own—anything whatever, whether book or tablets or pen or whatever it may be—since they are not permitted to have even their bodies or wills at their own disposal; but for all their necessities let them look to the Father of the monastery. And let it be unlawful to have anything which the Abbot has not given or allowed. Let all things be common to all, as it is written, and let no one say or assume that anything is his own.

But if anyone is caught indulging in this most wicked vice, let him be admonished once and a second time. If he fails to amend, let him undergo punishment.

CHAPTER 34

WHETHER ALL SHOULD RECEIVE IN EQUAL MEASURE WHAT IS NECESSARY

Mar. 12—July 12—Nov. 11

Let us follow the Scripture, "Distribution was made to each according as anyone had need." By this we do not mean that there should be respecting of persons (which God forbid), but consideration for infirmities. He who needs less should thank God and not be discontented; but he who needs more should be humbled by the thought of his infirmity rather than feeling important on account of the kindness shown him. Thus all the members will be at peace.

Above all, let not the evil of murmuring appear for any reason whatsoever in the least word or sign. If anyone is caught at it, let him be placed under very severe discipline.

CHAPTER 35

ON THE WEEKLY SERVERS IN THE KITCHEN

Mar. 13—July 13—Nov. 12

Let the brethren serve one another, and let no one be excused from the kitchen service except by reason of sickness or occupation in some important work. For this service brings increase of reward and of charity. But let helpers be provided for the weak ones, that they may not be distressed by this work; and indeed let everyone have help, as required by the size of the community or the circumstances of the locality. If the community is a large one, the cellarer shall be excused from the kitchen service; and so also those whose occupations are of greater utility, as we said above. Let the rest serve one another in charity.

The one who is ending his week of service shall do the cleaning on Saturday. He shall wash the towels with which the brethren wipe their hands and feet; and this server who is ending his week, aided by the one who is about to begin, shall wash the feet of all the brethren. He shall return the utensils of his office to the cellarer clean and in good condition, and the cellarer in turn shall consign them to the incoming server, in order that he may know what he gives out and what he receives back.

Mar. 14—July 14—Nov. 13

An hour before the meal let the weekly servers each receive a drink and some bread, over and above the appointed allowance, in order that at the meal time they may serve their brethren without murmuring and without excessive fatigue. On solemn days, however, let them wait until after Mass.

Immediately after the Morning Office on Sunday, the incoming and outgoing servers shall prostrate themselves before all the brethren in the oratory and ask their prayers. Let the server who is ending his week say this verse: "Blessed are You, O Lord God, who have helped me and consoled me." When this has been said three times and the outgoing server has received his blessing, then let the incoming server follow and say, "Incline unto my aid, O God; O Lord, make haste to help me." Let this also be repeated three times by all, and having received his blessing let him enter his service.

CHAPTER 36

ON THE SICK BRETHREN

Mar. 15—July 15—Nov. 14

Before all things and above all things, care must be taken of the sick, so that they will be served as if they were Christ in person; for He Himself said, "I was sick, and you visited Me," and, "What you did for one of these least ones, you did for Me." But let the sick on their part consider that they are being served for the honor of God, and let them not annoy their brethren who are serving them by their unnecessary demands. Yet they should be patiently borne with, because from such as these is gained a more abundant reward. Therefore the Abbot shall take the greatest care that they suffer no neglect.

For these sick brethren let there be assigned a special room and an attendant who is God-fearing, diligent and solicitous. Let the use of baths be afforded the sick as often as may be expedient;

but to the healthy, and especially to the young, let them be granted more rarely. Moreover, let the use of meat be granted to the sick who are very weak, for the restoration of their strength; but when they are convalescent, let all abstain from meat as usual.

The Abbot shall take the greatest care that the sick be not neglected by the cellarers or the attendants; for he also is responsible for what is done wrongly by his disciples.

CHAPTER 37

ON OLD MEN AND CHILDREN

Mar. 16—July 16—Nov. 15

Although human nature itself is drawn to special kindness towards these times of life, that is towards old men and children, still the authority of the Rule should also provide for them. Let their weakness be always taken into account, and let them by no means be held to the rigor of the Rule with regard to food. On the contrary, let a kind consideration be shown to them, and let them eat before the regular hours.

CHAPTER 38

ON THE WEEKLY READER

Mar. 17—July 17—Nov. 16

The meals of the brethren should not be without reading. Nor should the reader be anyone who happens to take up the book; but there should be a reader for the whole week, entering that office on Sunday. Let this incoming reader, after Mass and Communion, ask all to pray for him that God may keep him from the spirit of pride. And let him intone the following verse, which shall be said three times by all in the oratory: "O Lord, open my lips, and my mouth shall declare Your praise." Then, having received a blessing, let him enter on the reading.

And let absolute silence be kept at table, so that no whispering may be heard nor any voice except the reader's. As to the things they need while they eat and drink, let the brethren pass them to one another so that no one need ask for anything. If anything is needed, however, let it be asked for by means of some audible sign rather than by speech. Nor shall anyone at table presume to ask questions about the reading or anything else, lest that give occasion for talking; except that the Superior may perhaps wish to say something briefly for the purpose of edification.

The brother who is reader for the week shall take a little refreshment before he begins to read, on account of the Holy Communion and lest perhaps the fast be hard for him to bear. He shall take his meal afterwards with the kitchen and table servers of the week.

The brethren are not to read or chant in order, but only those who edify their hearers.

CHAPTER 39

ON THE MEASURE OF FOOD

Mar. 18—July 18—Nov. 17

We think it sufficient for the daily dinner, whether at the sixth or the ninth hour, that every table have two cooked dishes, on account of individual infirmities, so that he who for some reason cannot eat of the one may make his meal of the other. Therefore let two cooked dishes suffice for all the brethren; and if any fruit or fresh vegetables are available, let a third dish be added.

Let a good pound weight of bread suffice for the day, whether there be only one meal or both dinner and supper. If they are to have supper, the cellarer shall reserve a third of that pound, to be given them at supper.

But if it happens that the work was heavier, it shall lie within the Abbot's discretion and power, should it be expedient, to add something to the fare. Above all things, however, over-indulgence must be avoided and a monk must never be overtaken by indigestion; for there is nothing so opposed to the Christian character as over-indulgence, according to Our Lord's words, "See to it that your hearts be not burdened with over-indulgence."

Young boys shall not receive the same amount of food as their elders, but less; and frugality shall be observed in all circumstances.

Except the sick who are very weak, let all abstain entirely from eating the flesh of four-footed animals.

CHAPTER 40

ON THE MEASURE OF DRINK

Mar. 19—July 19—Nov. 18

"Everyone has his own gift from God, one in this way and another in that." It is therefore with some misgiving that we regulate the measure of other men's sustenance. Nevertheless, keeping in view the needs of weaker brethren, we believe that a hemina of wine a day is sufficient for each. But those to whom God gives the strength to abstain should know that they will receive a special reward.

If the circumstances of the place, or the work, or the heat of summer require a greater measure, the Superior shall use his judgment in the matter, taking care always that there be no occasion for surfeit or drunkenness. We read, it is true, that wine is by no means a drink for monks; but since the monks of our day cannot be persuaded of this, let us at least agree to drink sparingly and not to satiety, because "wine makes even the wise fall away."

But where the circumstances of the place are such that not even the measure prescribed above can be supplied, but much less or none at all, let those who live there bless God and not murmur. Above all things do we give this admonition, that they abstain from murmuring.

CHAPTER 41

AT WHAT HOURS THE MEALS SHOULD BE TAKEN

Mar. 20—July 20—Nov. 19

From holy Easter until Pentecost let the brethren take dinner at the sixth hour and supper in the evening.

From Pentecost throughout the summer, unless the monks have work in the fields or the excessive heat of summer oppresses them, let them fast on Wednesdays and Fridays until the ninth hour; on the other days let them dine at the sixth hour. This dinner at the sixth hour shall be the daily schedule if they have work in the fields or the heat of summer is extreme; the Abbot's foresight shall decide on this. Thus it is that he should adapt and arrange everything in such a way that souls may be saved and that the brethren may do their work without just cause for murmuring.

From the Ides of September until the beginning of Lent let them always take their dinner at the ninth hour.

In Lent until Easter let them dine in the evening. But this evening hour shall be so determined that they will not need the light of a lamp while eating, but everything will be accomplished while it is still daylight. Indeed at all seasons let the hour, whether for supper or for dinner, be so arranged that everything will be done by daylight.

CHAPTER 42

THAT NO ONE SPEAK AFTER COMPLINE

Mar. 21—July 21—Nov. 20

Monks ought to be zealous for silence at all times, but especially during the hours of the night. For every season, therefore, whether there be fasting or two meals, let the program be as follows:

If it be a season when there are two meals, then as soon as they have risen from supper they shall all sit together, and one of them shall read the Conferences or the Lives of the Fathers or something else that may edify the hearers; not the Heptateuch or the Books of Kings, however, because it will not be expedient for weak minds to hear those parts of Scripture at that hour; but they shall be read at other times.

If it be a day of fast, then having allowed a short interval after Vespers they shall proceed at once to the reading of the Conferences, as prescribed above; four or five pages being read, or as much as time permits, so that during the delay provided by this reading all may come together, including those who may have been occupied in some work assigned them.

When all, therefore, are gathered together, let them say Compline; and when they come out from Compline, no one shall be allowed to say anything from that time on. And if anyone should be found evading this rule of silence, let him undergo severe punishment. An exception shall be made if the need of speaking to guests should arise or if the Abbot should give someone an order. But even this should be done with the utmost gravity and the most becoming restraint.

CHAPTER 43

ON THOSE WHO COME LATE TO THE WORK OF GOD OR TO TABLE

Mar. 22—July 22—Nov. 21

At the hour for the Divine Office, as soon as the signal is heard, let them abandon whatever they may have in hand and hasten with the greatest speed, yet with seriousness, so that there is no excuse for levity. Let nothing, therefore, be put before the Work of God.

If at the Night Office anyone arrives after the "Glory be to the Father" of Psalm 94—which Psalm for this reason we wish to be said very slowly and protractedly—let him not stand in his usual place in the choir; but let him stand last of all, or in a place set aside by the Abbot for such negligent

ones in order that they may be seen by him and
by all. He shall remain there until the Work of
God has been completed, and then do penance
by a public satisfaction. The reason why we have
judged it fitting for them to stand in the last place
or in a place apart is that, being seen by all, they
may amend for very shame. For if they remain
outside of the oratory, there will perhaps be
someone who will go back to bed and sleep or at
least seat himself outside and indulge in idle talk,
and thus an occasion will be provided for the evil
one. But let them go inside, that they may not lose
the whole Office, and may amend for the future.

At the day Hours anyone who does not arrive
at the Work of God until after the verse and
the "Glory be to the Father" of the first Psalm
following it shall stand in the last place, according
to our ruling above. Nor shall he presume to join
the choir in their chanting until he has made
satisfaction, unless the Abbot should pardon
him and give him permission; but even then the
offender must make satisfaction for his fault.

Mar. 23—July 23—Nov. 22

Anyone who does not come to table before the
verse, so that all together may say the verse and

the oration and all sit down to table at the same time—anyone who through his own carelessness or bad habit does not come on time shall be corrected for this up to the second time. If then he does not amend, he shall not be allowed to share in the common table, but shall be separated from the company of all and made to eat alone, and his portion of wine shall be taken away from him, until he has made satisfaction and has amended. And let him suffer a like penalty who is not present at the verse said after the meal.

And let no one presume to take any food or drink before or after the appointed time. But if anyone is offered something by the Superior and refuses to take it, then when the time comes that he desires what he formerly refused or something else, let him receive nothing whatever until he has made proper satisfaction.

CHAPTER 44

HOW THE EXCOMMUNICATED ARE TO MAKE SATISFACTION

Mar. 24—July 24—Nov. 23

One who for serious faults is excommunicated from oratory and table shall make satisfaction as follows. At the hour when the celebration of the Work of God is concluded in the oratory, let him lie prostrate before the door of the oratory, saying nothing, but only lying prone with his face to the ground at the feet of all as they come out of the oratory. And let him continue to do this until the Abbot judges that satisfaction has been made. Then, when he has come at the Abbot's bidding, let him cast himself first at the Abbot's feet and then at the feet of all, that they may pray for him.

And next, if the Abbot so orders, let him be received into the choir, to the place which the Abbot appoints, but with the provision that he shall not presume to intone Psalm or lesson or anything else in the oratory without a further order from the Abbot. Moreover, at every Hour, when the Work of God is ended, let him cast himself on the ground in the place where he stands. And let him continue to satisfy in this way until the Abbot again orders him finally to cease from this satisfaction.

But those who for slight faults are excommunicated only from table shall make satisfaction in the oratory, and continue in it till an order from the Abbot, until he blesses them and says, "It is enough."

CHAPTER 45

ON THOSE WHO MAKE MISTAKES IN THE ORATORY

Mar. 25—July 25—Nov. 24

When anyone has made a mistake while reciting a Psalm, a responsory, an antiphon or a lesson, if he does not humble himself there before all by making a satisfaction, let him undergo a greater punishment because he would not correct by humility what he did wrong through carelessness.

But boys for such faults shall be whipped.

CHAPTER 46

ON THOSE WHO FAIL IN ANY OTHER MATTERS

Mar. 26—July 26—Nov. 25

When anyone is engaged in any sort of work, whether in the kitchen, in the cellar, in a shop, in the bakery, in the garden, while working at some craft, or in any other place, and he commits some fault, or breaks something, or loses something, or transgresses in any other way whatsoever, if he does not come immediately before the Abbot and the community of his own accord to make satisfaction and confess his fault, then when it becomes known through another, let him be subjected to a more severe correction.

But if the sin-sickness of the soul is a hidden one, let him reveal it only to the Abbot or to a spiritual father, who knows how to cure his own and others' wounds without exposing them and making them public.

CHAPTER 47

ON GIVING THE SIGNAL FOR THE TIME OF THE WORK OF GOD

Mar. 27—July 27—Nov. 26

The indicating of the hour of the Work of God by day and by night shall devolve upon the Abbot, either to give the signal himself or to assign this duty to such a careful brother that everything will take place at the proper hours.

Let the Psalms and the antiphons be intoned by those who are appointed for it, in their order after the Abbot. And no one shall presume to sing or read unless he can fulfil that office in such a way as to edify the hearers. Let this function be performed with humility, gravity and reverence, and by him whom the Abbot has appointed.

CHAPTER 48

ON THE DAILY MANUAL LABOR

Mar. 28—July 28—Nov. 27

Idleness is the enemy of the soul. Therefore the brethren should be occupied at certain times in manual labor, and again at fixed hours in sacred reading. To that end we think that the times for each may be prescribed as follows.

From Easter until the Calends of October, when they come out from Prime in the morning let them labor at whatever is necessary until about the fourth hour, and from the fourth hour until about the sixth let them apply themselves to reading. After the sixth hour, having left the table, let them rest on their beds in perfect silence; or if anyone may perhaps want to read, let him read to himself in such a way as not to disturb anyone else. Let None be said rather early, at the middle of the eighth hour, and let them again do what work has to be done until Vespers.

And if the circumstances of the place or their poverty should require that they themselves do the work of gathering the harvest, let them not be discontented; for then are they truly monks when they live by the labor of their hands, as did our Fathers and the Apostles. Let all things be done with moderation, however, for the sake of the faint-hearted.

Mar. 29—July 29—Nov. 28

From the Calends of October until the beginning of Lent, let them apply themselves to reading up to the end of the second hour. At the second hour let Terce be said, and then let all labor at the work assigned them until None. At the first signal for the Hour of None let everyone break off from his work, and hold himself ready for the sounding of the second signal. After the meal let them apply themselves to their reading or to the Psalms.

On the days of Lent, from morning until the end of the third hour let them apply themselves to their reading, and from then until the end of the tenth hour let them do the work assigned them. And in these days of Lent they shall each receive a book from the library, which they shall read straight through from the beginning. These books are to be given out at the beginning of Lent.

But certainly one or two of the seniors should be deputed to go about the monastery at the hours when the brethren are occupied in reading and see that there be no lazy brother who spends his time in idleness or gossip and does not apply himself to the reading, so that he is not only unprofitable to himself but also distracts others. If such a one be found (which God forbid), let him be corrected once and a second time; if he does not amend, let him undergo the punishment of the Rule in such a way that the rest may take warning.

Moreover, one brother shall not associate with another at unseasonable hours.

Mar. 30—July 30—Nov. 29

On Sundays, let all occupy themselves in reading, except those who have been appointed to various duties. But if anyone should be so negligent and shiftless that he will not or cannot study or read, let him be given some work to do so that he will not be idle.

Weak or sickly brethren should be assigned a task or craft of such a nature as to keep them from idleness and at the same time not to overburden them or drive them away with excessive toil. Their weakness must be taken into consideration by the Abbot.

CHAPTER 49

ON THE OBSERVANCE OF LENT

Mar. 31—July 31—Nov. 30

Although the life of a monk ought to have about it at all times the character of a Lenten observance, yet since few have the virtue for that, we therefore urge that during the actual days of Lent the brethren keep their lives most pure and at the same time wash away during these holy days all the negligences of other times. And this will be worthily done if we restrain ourselves from all vices and give ourselves up to prayer with tears, to reading, to compunction of heart and to abstinence.

During these days, therefore, let us increase somewhat the usual burden of our service, as by private prayers and by abstinence in food and drink. Thus everyone of his own will may offer

God "with joy of the Holy Spirit" something above the measure required of him. From his body, that is, he may withhold some food, drink, sleep, talking and jesting; and with the joy of spiritual desire he may look forward to holy Easter.

Let each one, however, suggest to his Abbot what it is that he wants to offer, and let it be done with his blessing and approval. For anything done without the permission of the spiritual father will be imputed to presumption and vainglory and will merit no reward. Therefore let everything be done with the Abbot's approval.

CHAPTER 50

ON BRETHREN WHO ARE WORKING FAR FROM THE ORATORY OR ARE ON A JOURNEY

Apr. 1—Aug. 1—Dec. 1

Those brethren who are working at a great distance and cannot get to the oratory at the proper time—the Abbot judging that such is the case—shall perform the Work of God in the place where they are working, bending their knees in reverence before God.

Likewise those who have been sent on a journey shall not let the appointed Hours pass by, but shall say the Office by themselves as well as they can, and not neglect to render the task of their service.

CHAPTER 51

ON BRETHREN WHO GO NOT VERY FAR AWAY

Apr. 2—Aug. 2—Dec. 2

A brother who is sent out on some business and is expected to return to the monastery that same day shall not presume to eat while he is out, even if he is urgently requested to do so by any person whomsoever, unless he has permission from his Abbot. And if he acts otherwise, let him be excommunicated.

CHAPTER 52

ON THE ORATORY OF THE MONASTERY

Apr. 3—Aug. 3—Dec. 3

Let the oratory be what it is called, a place of prayer; and let nothing else be done there or kept there. When the Work of God is ended, let all go out in perfect silence, and let reverence for God be observed, so that any brother who may wish to pray privately will not be hindered by another's misconduct. And at other times also, if anyone should want to pray by himself, let him go in simply and pray, not in a loud voice but with tears and fervor of heart. He who does not say his prayers in this way, therefore, shall not be permitted to remain in the oratory when the Work of God is ended, lest another be hindered, as we have said.

CHAPTER 53

ON THE RECEPTION OF GUESTS

Apr. 4—Aug. 4—Dec. 4

Let all guests who arrive be received like Christ, for He is going to say, "I came as a guest, and you received Me." And to all let due honor be shown, especially to the domestics of the faith and to pilgrims.

As soon as a guest is announced, therefore, let the Superior or the brethren meet him with all charitable service. And first of all let them pray together, and then exchange the kiss of peace. For the kiss of peace should not be offered until after the prayers have been said, on account of the devil's deceptions.

In the salutation of all guests, whether arriving or departing, let all humility be shown. Let the head be bowed or the whole body prostrated on the ground in adoration of Christ, who indeed is received in their persons.

After the guests have been received and taken to prayer, let the Superior or someone appointed by him sit with them. Let the divine law be read before the guest for his edification, and then let all kindness be shown him. The Superior shall break his fast for the sake of a guest, unless it happens to be a principal fast day which may not be violated. The brethren, however, shall observe the customary fasts. Let the Abbot give the guests water for their hands; and let both Abbot and community wash the feet of all guests. After the washing of the feet let them say this verse: "We have received Your mercy, O God, in the midst of Your temple."

In the reception of the poor and of pilgrims the greatest care and solicitude should be shown, because it is especially in them that Christ is received; for as far as the rich are concerned, the very fear which they inspire wins respect for them.

Apr. 5—Aug. 5—Dec. 5

Let there be a separate kitchen for the Abbot and guests, that the brethren may not be disturbed when guests, who are never lacking in a monastery, arrive at irregular hours. Let two brethren capable of filling the office well be appointed for a year to have charge of this kitchen. Let them be given such help as they need, that they may serve without murmuring. And on the other hand, when they have less to occupy them, let them go out to whatever work is assigned them.

And not only in their case but in all the offices of the monastery let this arrangement be observed, that when help is needed it be supplied, and again when the workers are unoccupied they do whatever they are bidden.

The guest house also shall be assigned to a brother whose soul is possessed by the fear of God. Let there be a sufficient number of beds made up in it; and let the house of God be managed by prudent men and in a prudent manner.

On no account shall anyone who is not so ordered associate or converse with guests. But if he should meet them or see them, let him greet them humbly, as we have said, ask their blessing and pass on, saying that he is not allowed to converse with a guest.

CHAPTER 54

WHETHER A MONK SHOULD RECEIVE LETTERS OR ANYTHING ELSE

Apr. 6—Aug. 6—Dec. 6

On no account shall a monk be allowed to receive letters, tokens or any little gift whatsoever from his parents or anyone else, or from his brethren, or to give the same, without the Abbot's permission. But if anything is sent him even by his parents, let him not presume to take it before it has been shown to the Abbot. And it shall be in the Abbot's power to decide to whom it shall be given, if he allows it to be received; and the brother to whom it was sent should not be grieved, lest occasion be given to the devil.

Should anyone presume to act otherwise, let him undergo the discipline of the Rule.

CHAPTER 55

ON THE CLOTHES AND SHOES OF THE BRETHREN

Apr. 7—Aug. 7—Dec. 7

Let clothing be given to the brethren according to the nature of the place in which they dwell and its climate; for in cold regions more will be needed, and in warm regions less. This is to be taken into consideration, therefore, by the Abbot.

We believe, however, that in ordinary places the following dress is sufficient for each monk: a tunic, a cowl (thick and woolly for winter, thin or worn for summer), a scapular for work, stockings and shoes to cover the feet.

The monks should not complain about the color or the coarseness of any of these things, but be content with what can be found in the district where they live and can be purchased cheaply.

The Abbot shall see to the size of the garments, that they be not too short for those who wear them, but of the proper fit.

Let those who receive new clothes always give back the old ones at once, to be put away in the wardrobe for the poor. For it is sufficient if a monk has two tunics and two cowls, to allow for night wear and for the washing of these garments; more than that is superfluity and should be taken away. Let them return their stockings also and anything else that is old when they receive new ones.

Those who are sent on a journey shall receive drawers from the wardrobe, which they shall wash and restore on their return. And let their cowls and tunics be somewhat better than what they usually wear. These they shall receive from the wardrobe when they set out on a journey, and restore when they return.

Apr. 8—Aug. 8—Dec. 8

For bedding let this suffice: a mattress, a blanket, a coverlet and a pillow.

The beds, moreover, are to be examined frequently by the Abbot, to see if any private property be found in them. If anyone should be found to have something that he did not receive from the Abbot, let him undergo the most severe discipline.

And in order that this vice of private ownership may be cut out by the roots, the Abbot should provide all the necessary articles: cowl, tunic, stockings, shoes, girdle, knife, pen, needle, handkerchief, tablets; that all pretext of need may be taken away. Yet the Abbot should always keep in mind the sentence from the Acts of the Apostles that "distribution was made to each according as anyone had need." In this manner, therefore, let the Abbot consider the weaknesses of the needy and not the ill-will of the envious. But in all his decisions let him think about the retribution of God.

CHAPTER 56

ON THE ABBOT'S TABLE

Apr. 9—Aug. 9—Dec. 9

Let the Abbot's table always be with the guests and the pilgrims. But when there are no guests, let it be in his power to invite whom he will of the brethren. Yet one or two seniors must always be left with the brethren for the sake of discipline.

CHAPTER 57

ON THE CRAFTSMEN OF THE MONASTERY

Apr. 10—Aug. 10—Dec. 10

If there are craftsmen in the monastery, let them practice their crafts with all humility, provided the Abbot has given permission. But if any one of them becomes conceited over his skill in his craft, because he seems to be conferring a benefit on the monastery, let him be taken from his craft and no longer exercise it unless, after he has humbled himself, the Abbot again gives him permission.

If any of the work of the craftsmen is to be sold, let those through whose hands the transactions pass see to it that they do not presume to practice any fraud. Let them always remember Ananias and Saphira, lest perhaps the death which these incurred in the body, they themselves and any others who would deal

dishonestly with the monastery's property should
suffer in the soul. And in the prices let not the
sin of avarice creep in, but let the goods always
be sold a little cheaper than they can be sold by
people in the world, "that in all things God may be
glorified."

CHAPTER 58

ON THE MANNER OF RECEIVING BRETHREN

Apr. 11—Aug. 11—Dec. 11

When anyone is newly come for the reformation of his life, let him not be granted an easy entrance; but, as the Apostle says, "Test the spirits to see whether they are from God." If the newcomer, therefore, perseveres in his knocking, and if it is seen after four or five days that he bears patiently the harsh treatment offered him and the difficulty of admission, and that he persists in his petition, then let entrance be granted him, and let him stay in the guest house for a few days.

After that let him live in the novitiate, where the novices study, eat and sleep. A senior shall be assigned to them who is skilled in winning souls, to watch over them with the utmost care. Let him examine whether the novice is truly seeking God, and whether he is zealous for the Work of God, for obedience and for humiliations. Let the novice be told all the hard and rugged ways by which the journey to God is made.

If he promises stability and perseverance, then at the end of two months let this Rule be read through to him, and let him be addressed thus: "Here is the law under which you wish to fight. If you can observe it, enter; if you cannot, you are free to depart." If he still stands firm, let him be taken to the above-mentioned novitiate and again tested in all patience. And after the lapse of six months let the Rule be read to him, that he may know on what he is entering. And if he still remains firm, after four months let the same Rule be read to him again.

Then, having deliberated with himself, if he promises to keep it in its entirety and to observe everything that is commanded him, let him be received into the community. But let him understand that, according to the law of the Rule, from that day forward he may not leave the monastery nor withdraw his neck from under the yoke of the Rule which he was free to refuse or to accept during that prolonged deliberation.

Apr. 12—Aug. 12—Dec. 12

He who is to be received shall make a promise before all in the oratory of his stability and of the reformation of his life and of obedience.

This promise he shall make before God and His Saints, so that if he should ever act otherwise, he may know that he will be condemned by Him whom he mocks. Of this promise of his let him draw up a petition in the name of the Saints whose relics are there and of the Abbot who is present. Let him write this petition with his own hand; or if he is illiterate, let another write it at his request, and let the novice put his mark to it. Then let him place it with his own hand upon the altar; and when he has placed it there, let the novice at once intone this verse: "Receive me, O Lord, according to Your word, and I shall live: and let me not be confounded in my hope." Let the whole community answer this verse three times and add the "Glory be to the Father." Then let the novice brother prostrate himself at each one's feet, that they may pray for him. And from that day forward let him be counted as one of the community.

If he has any property, let him either give it beforehand to the poor or by solemn donation bestow it on the monastery, reserving nothing at all for himself, as indeed he knows that from that day forward he will no longer have power even over his own body. At once, therefore, in the oratory, let him be divested of his own clothes which he is wearing and dressed in the clothes of the monastery. But let the clothes of which he was divested be put aside in the wardrobe and kept there. Then if he should ever listen to the persuasions of the devil and decide to leave the monastery (which God forbid), he may be divested of the monastic clothes and cast out. His petition, however, which the Abbot has taken from the altar, shall not be returned to him, but shall be kept in the monastery.

CHAPTER 59

ON THE SONS OF NOBLES AND OF THE POOR WHO ARE OFFERED

Apr. 13—Aug. 13—Dec. 13

If anyone of the nobility offers his son to God in the monastery and the boy is very young, let his parents draw up the petition which we mentioned above; and at the oblation let them wrap the petition and the boy's hand in the altar cloth and so offer him.

As regards their property, they shall promise in the same petition under oath that they will never of themselves, or through an intermediary, or in any way whatever, give him anything or provide him with the opportunity of owning anything. Or else, if they are unwilling to do this, and if they want to offer something as an alms to the monastery for their advantage, let them make a donation of the property they wish to give to the monastery, reserving the income to themselves if they wish. And in this way let everything be barred, so that the boy may have no expectations whereby (which God forbid) he might be deceived and ruined, as we have learned by experience.

Let those who are less well-to-do make a similar offering. But those who have nothing at all shall simply draw up the petition and offer their son before witnesses at the oblation.

CHAPTER 60

ON PRIESTS WHO MAY WISH TO LIVE IN THE MONASTERY

Apr. 14—Aug. 14—Dec. 14

If anyone of the priestly order should ask to be received into the monastery, permission shall not be granted him too readily. But if he is quite persistent in his request, let him know that he will have to observe the whole discipline of the Rule and that nothing will be relaxed in his favor, that it may be as it is written: "Friend, for what have you come?"

It shall be granted him, however, to stand next after the Abbot and to give blessings and to celebrate Mass, but only by order of the Abbot. Without such order let him not presume to do anything, knowing that he is subject to the discipline of the Rule; but rather let him give an example of humility to all.

If there happens to be question of an appointment or of some business in the monastery, let him expect the rank due him according to the date of his entrance into the monastery, and not the place granted him out of reverence for the priesthood.

If any clerics, moved by the same desire, should wish to join the monastery, let them be placed in a middle rank. But they too are to be admitted only if they promise observance of the Rule and their own stability.

CHAPTER 61

HOW PILGRIM MONKS ARE TO BE RECEIVED

Apr. 15—Aug. 15—Dec. 15

If a pilgrim monk coming from a distant region wants to live as a guest of the monastery, let him be received for as long a time as he desires, provided he is content with the customs of the place as he finds them and does not disturb the monastery by superfluous demands, but is simply content with what he finds. If, however, he censures or points out anything reasonably and with the humility of charity, let the Abbot consider prudently whether perhaps it was for that very purpose that the Lord sent him.

If afterwards he should want to bind himself
to stability, his wish should not be denied him,
especially since there has been opportunity during
his stay as a guest to discover his character.

Apr. 16—Aug. 16—Dec. 16

But if as a guest he was found exacting or prone
to vice, not only should he be denied membership
in the community, but he should even be politely
requested to leave, lest others be corrupted by his
evil life.

If, however, he has not proved to be the kind
who deserves to be put out, he should not only on
his own application be received as a member of
the community, but he should even be persuaded
to stay, that the others may be instructed by his
example, and because in every place it is the same
Lord who is served, the same King for whom the
battle is fought.

Moreover, if the Abbot perceives that he is a
worthy man, he may put him in a somewhat higher
rank. And not only with regard to a monk but also
with regard to those in priestly or clerical orders
previously mentioned, the Abbot may establish them
in a higher rank than would be theirs by date of

entrance if he perceives that their life is deserving.

Let the Abbot take care, however, never to receive a monk from another known monastery as a member of his community without the consent of his Abbot or a letter of recommendation; for it is written, "Do not to another what you would not want done to yourself."

CHAPTER 62

ON THE PRIESTS OF THE MONASTERY

Apr. 17—Aug. 17—Dec. 17

If an Abbot desire to have a priest or a deacon ordained for his monastery, let him choose one of his monks who is worthy to exercise the priestly office.

But let the one who is ordained beware of self-exaltation or pride; and let him not presume to do anything except what is commanded him by the Abbot, knowing that he is so much the more subject to the discipline of the Rule. Nor should he by reason of his priesthood forget the obedience and the discipline required by the Rule, but make ever more and more progress towards God.

Let him always keep the place which he received on entering the monastery, except in his duties at the altar or in case the choice of the community and the will of the Abbot should promote him for the worthiness of his life. Yet he must understand that he is to observe the rules laid down by deans and Priors.

Should he presume to act otherwise, let him be judged not as a priest but as a rebel. And if he does not reform after repeated admonitions, let even the Bishop be brought in as a witness. If then he still fails to amend, and his offences are notorious, let him be put out of the monastery, but only if his contumacy is such that he refuses to submit or to obey the Rule.

CHAPTER 63

ON THE ORDER OF THE COMMUNITY

Apr. 18—Aug. 18—Dec. 18

Let all keep their places in the monastery established by the time of their entrance, the merit of their lives and the decision of the Abbot. Yet the Abbot must not disturb the flock committed to him, nor by an arbitrary use of his power ordain anything unjustly; but let him always think of the account he will have to render to God for all his decisions and his deeds.

Therefore in that order which he has established or which they already had, let the brethren approach to receive the kiss of peace and Communion, intone the Psalms and stand in choir. And in no place whatever should age decide the order or be prejudicial to it; for Samuel and Daniel as mere boys judged priests.

Except for those already mentioned, therefore, whom the Abbot has promoted by a special decision or demoted for definite reasons, all the rest shall take their order according to the time of their entrance. Thus, for example, he who came to the monastery at the second hour of the day, whatever be his age or his dignity, must know that he is junior to one who came at the first hour of the day. Boys, however, are to be kept under discipline in all matters and by everyone.

Apr. 19—Aug. 19—Dec. 19

The juniors, therefore, should honor their seniors, and the seniors love their juniors.

In the very manner of address, let no one call another by the mere name; but let the seniors call their juniors Brothers, and the juniors call their seniors Fathers, by which is conveyed the reverence due to a father. But the Abbot, since he is believed to represent Christ, shall be called Lord and Abbot, not for any pretensions of his own but out of honor and love for Christ. Let the Abbot himself reflect on this, and show himself worthy of such an honor.

And wherever the brethren meet one another the junior shall ask the senior for his blessing.

When a senior passes by, a junior shall rise and give him a place to sit, nor shall the junior presume to sit with him unless his senior bid him, that it may be as was written, "In honor anticipating one another."

Boys, both small and adolescent, shall keep strictly to their rank in oratory and at table. But outside of that, wherever they may be, let them be under supervision and discipline, until they come to the age of discretion.

CHAPTER 64

ON CONSTITUTING
AN ABBOT

Apr. 20—Aug. 20—Dec. 20

In the constituting of an Abbot let this plan always be followed, that the office be conferred on the one who is chosen either by the whole community unanimously in the fear of God or else by a part of the community, however small, if its counsel is more wholesome.

Merit of life and wisdom of doctrine should determine the choice of the one to be constituted, even if he be the last in the order of the community.

But if (which God forbid) the whole community should agree to choose a person who will acquiesce in their vices, and if those vices somehow become known to the Bishop to whose diocese the place belongs, or to the Abbots or the faithful of the vicinity, let them prevent the success of this conspiracy of the wicked, and set a worthy steward over the house of God. They may be sure that they will receive a good reward for this action if they do it with a pure intention and out of zeal for God; as, on the contrary, they will sin if they fail to do it.

Apr. 21—Aug. 21—Dec. 21

Once he has been constituted, let the Abbot always bear in mind what a burden he has undertaken and to whom he will have to give an account of his stewardship, and let him know that his duty is rather to profit his brethren than to preside over them. He must therefore be learned in the divine law, that he may have a treasure of knowledge from which to bring forth new things and old. He must be chaste, sober and merciful. Let him exalt mercy above judgment, that he himself may obtain mercy. He should hate vices; he should love the brethren.

In administering correction he should act prudently and not go to excess, lest in seeking too eagerly to scrape off the rust he break the vessel. Let him keep his own frailty ever before his eyes and remember that the bruised reed must not be broken. By this we do not mean that he should allow vices to grow; on the contrary, as we have already said, he should eradicate them prudently and with charity, in the way which may seem best in each case. Let him study rather to be loved than to be feared.

Let him not be excitable and worried, nor exacting and headstrong, nor jealous and over-suspicious; for then he is never at rest.

In his commands let him be prudent and considerate; and whether the work which he enjoins concerns God or the world, let him be discreet and moderate, bearing in mind the discretion of holy Jacob, who said, "If I cause my flocks to be overdriven, they will all die in one day." Taking this, then, and other examples of discretion, the mother of virtues, let him so temper all things that the strong may have something to strive after, and the weak may not fall back in dismay.

And especially let him keep this Rule in all its details, so that after a good ministry he may hear from the Lord what the good servant heard who gave his fellow-servants wheat in due season: "Indeed, I tell you, he will set him over all his goods."

CHAPTER 65

ON THE PRIOR OF THE MONASTERY

Apr. 22—Aug. 22—Dec. 22

It happens all too often that the constituting of a Prior gives rise to grave scandals in monasteries. For there are some who become inflated with the evil spirit of pride and consider themselves second Abbots. By usurping power they foster scandals and cause dissensions in the community. Especially does this happen in those places where the Prior is constituted by the same Bishop or the same Abbots who constitute the Abbot himself. What an absurd procedure this is can easily be seen; for it gives the Prior an occasion for becoming proud from the very time of his constitution, by putting the thought into his mind that he is freed from the authority of his Abbot: "For," he will say to himself, "you were constituted by the same persons who constituted the Abbot." From this source are stirred up envy, quarrels, detraction, rivalry, dissensions and disorders. For while the Abbot and the Prior are at variance, their souls cannot but be endangered by this dissension; and those who are under them, currying favor with one side or the other, go to ruin. The guilt for this dangerous state of affairs rests on the heads of those whose action brought about such disorder.

Apr. 23—Aug. 23—Dec. 23

To us, therefore, it seems expedient for the preservation of peace and charity that the Abbot have in his hands the full administration of his monastery. And if possible let all the affairs of the monastery, as we have already arranged, be administered by deans according to the Abbot's directions. Thus, with the duties being shared by several, no one person will become proud.

But if the circumstances of the place require it, or if the community asks for it with reason and with humility, and the Abbot judges it to be expedient, let the Abbot himself constitute as his Prior whomsoever he shall choose with the counsel of God-fearing brethren.

That Prior, however, shall perform respectfully the duties enjoined on him by his Abbot and do nothing against the Abbot's will or direction; for the more he is raised above the rest, the more carefully should he observe the precepts of the Rule.

If it should be found that the Prior has serious faults, or that he is deceived by his exaltation and yields to pride, or if he should be proved to be a despiser of the Holy Rule, let him be admonished verbally up to four times. If he fails to amend, let the correction of regular discipline be applied to him. But if even then he does not reform, let him be deposed from the office of Prior and another be appointed in his place who is worthy of it. And if afterwards he is not quiet and obedient in the community, let him even be expelled from the monastery. But the Abbot, for his part, should bear in mind that he will have to render an account to God for all his judgments, lest the flame of envy or jealousy be kindled in his soul.

CHAPTER 66

ON THE PORTERS OF THE MONASTERY

Apr. 24—Aug. 24—Dec. 24

At the gate of the monastery let there be placed a wise old man, who knows how to receive and to give a message, and whose maturity will prevent him from straying about. This porter should have a room near the gate, so that those who come may always find someone at hand to attend to their business. And as soon as anyone knocks or a poor man hails him, let him answer, "Thanks be to God" or "A blessing!" Then let him attend to them promptly, with all the meekness inspired by the fear of God and with the warmth of charity.

Should the porter need help, let him have one of the younger brethren.

If it can be done, the monastery should be so established that all the necessary things, such as water, mill, garden and various workshops, may be within the enclosure, so that there is no necessity for the monks to go about outside of it, since that is not at all profitable for their souls.

We desire that this Rule be read often in the community, so that none of the brethren may excuse himself on the ground of ignorance.

CHAPTER 67

ON BRETHREN WHO ARE SENT ON A JOURNEY

Apr. 25—Aug. 25—Dec. 25

Let the brethren who are sent on a journey commend themselves to the prayers of all the brethren and of the Abbot; and always at the last prayer of the Work of God let a commemoration be made of all absent brethren.

When brethren return from a journey, at the end of each canonical Hour of the Work of God on the day they return, let them lie prostrate on the floor of the oratory and beg the prayers of all on account of any faults that may have surprised them on the road, through the seeing or hearing of something evil, or through idle talk. And let no one presume to tell another whatever he may have seen or heard outside of the monastery, because this causes very great harm. But if anyone presumes to do so, let him undergo the punishment of the Rule. And let him be punished likewise who would presume to leave the enclosure of the monastery and go anywhere or do anything, however small, without an order from the Abbot.

CHAPTER 68

IF A BROTHER IS COMMANDED TO DO IMPOSSIBLE THINGS

Apr. 26—Aug. 26—Dec. 26

If it happens that difficult or impossible tasks are laid on a brother, let him nevertheless receive the order of the one in authority with all meekness and obedience. But if he sees that the weight of the burden altogether exceeds the limit of his strength, let him submit the reasons for his inability to the one who is over him in a quiet way and at an opportune time, without pride, resistance, or contradiction. And if after these representations the Superior still persists in his decision and command, let the subject know that this is for his good, and let him obey out of love, trusting in the help of God.

CHAPTER 69

THAT THE MONKS PRESUME NOT TO DEFEND ONE ANOTHER

Apr. 27—Aug. 27—Dec. 27

Care must be taken that no monk presume on any ground to defend another monk in the monastery, or as it were to take him under his protection, even though they be united by some tie of blood-relationship. Let not the monks dare to do this in any way whatsoever, because it may give rise to most serious scandals. But if anyone breaks this rule, let him be severely punished.

CHAPTER 70

THAT NO ONE VENTURE TO PUNISH AT RANDOM

Apr. 28—Aug. 28—Dec. 28

Every occasion of presumption shall be avoided in the monastery, and we decree that no one be allowed to excommunicate or to strike any of his brethren unless the Abbot has given him the authority. Those who offend in this matter shall be rebuked in the presence of all, that the rest may have fear.

But boys up to 15 years of age shall be carefully controlled and watched by all, yet this too with all moderation and discretion. Anyone, therefore, who presumes without the Abbot's instructions to punish those above that age or who loses his temper with the boys, shall undergo the discipline of the Rule; for it is written, "Do not to another what you would not want done to yourself."

CHAPTER 71

THAT THE BRETHREN BE OBEDIENT TO ONE ANOTHER

Apr. 29—Aug. 29—Dec. 29

Not only is the boon of obedience to be shown by all to the Abbot, but the brethren are also to obey one another, knowing that by this road of obedience they are going to God. Giving priority, therefore, to the commands of the Abbot and of the Superiors appointed by him (to which we allow no private orders to be preferred), for the rest let all the juniors obey their seniors with all charity and solicitude. But if anyone is found contentious, let him be corrected.

And if any brother, for however small a cause, is corrected in any way by the Abbot or by any of his Superiors, or if he faintly perceives that the mind of any Superior is angered or moved against him, however little, let him at once, without delay, prostrate himself on the ground at his feet and lie there making satisfaction until that emotion is quieted with a blessing. But if anyone should disdain to do this, let him undergo corporal punishment or, if he is stubborn, let him be expelled from the monastery.

CHAPTER 72

ON THE GOOD ZEAL WHICH MONKS OUGHT TO HAVE

Apr. 30—Aug. 30—Dec. 30

Just as there is an evil zeal of bitterness which separates from God and leads to hell, so there is a good zeal which separates from vices and leads to God and to life everlasting. This zeal, therefore, the monks should practice with the most fervent love. Thus they should anticipate one another in honor; most patiently endure one another's infirmities, whether of body or of character; vie in paying obedience one to another—no one following what he considers useful for himself, but rather what benefits another—; tender the charity of brotherhood chastely; fear God in love; love

their Abbot with a sincere and humble charity;
prefer nothing whatever to Christ. And may He
bring us all together to life everlasting!

CHAPTER 73

ON THE FACT THAT THE FULL OBSERVANCE OF JUSTICE IS NOT ESTABLISHED IN THIS RULE

May 1—Aug. 31—Dec. 31

Now we have written this Rule in order that by its observance in monasteries we may show that we have attained some degree of virtue and the rudiments of the religious life.

But for him who would hasten to the perfection of that life there are the teachings of the holy Fathers, the observance of which leads a man to the height of perfection. For what page or what utterance of the divinely inspired books of the Old and New Testaments is not a most unerring rule for human life? Or what book of the holy Catholic Fathers does not loudly proclaim how we may come by a straight course to our Creator? Then the Conferences and the Institutes and the Lives of the Fathers, as also the Rule of our holy Father Basil—what else are they but tools of virtue for right-living and obedient monks? But for us who are lazy and ill-living and negligent they are a source of shame and confusion.

Whoever you are, therefore, who are hastening to the heavenly homeland, fulfil with the help of Christ this minimum Rule which we have written for beginners; and then at length under God's protection you will attain to the loftier heights of doctrine and virtue which we have mentioned above.